FATIMA

IN THE

THIRD MILLENNIUM

by
Timothy Tindal-Robertson

*All booklets are published thanks to the
generous support of the members of the
Catholic Truth Society*

CATHOLIC TRUTH SOCIETY
PUBLISHERS TO THE HOLY SEE

CONTENTS

INTRODUCTION

In the Holy Year 2000, Pope John Paul II carried out three acts of major importance with regard to Fatima which, when considered both individually and as a whole, have imparted significant new meaning to the message of Our Lady of Fatima, and which clearly demonstrate why and how it is more than ever relevant to the Church's mission of evangelisation in the opening century of the third millennium.

This study sets out to provide a straightforward account of these events and how they unfolded, so that in the new light which they shed upon it, we may seek to discern what is God's will for His Church, in her understanding and acceptance of Our Lady's message.

Pope John Paul II has stated that from the beginning of his pontificate his thoughts had been on the Holy Year 2000 "with the sole purpose of preparing everyone to be docile to the working of the Spirit" *(Incarnationis Mysterium, 2)*. Dedicated to the Incarnation of the Word, the Holy Year was intended to be intensely Eucharistic, as John Paul II wrote, in his Apostolic Letter *Novo Millennio Ineunte*, No. 11, issued on 6th January 2001. The Pope then continued:

'At the same time, along with the memory of the birth of the Son, how could the memory of the Mother be

missing ? Mary was present in the Jubilee celebration not
only as a theme of high-level academic gatherings, *but
above all in the great Act of Entrustment* (emphasis
added) with which, in the presence of a large part of the
world episcopate, I entrusted to her maternal care the
lives of the men and women of the new millennium.'

Acts of Entrustment

There had been several previous acts of entrustment to
the Blessed Virgin by John Paul II and Paul VI, but this
new act is distinguished from all previous ones by a quite
unique factor. Never before in history has a Pope solemn-
ly invoked the Mother's maternal protection and power of
intercession with her Son, on behalf of the Church, the
Bishops, and all mankind, *for the entire span of a millennium.* And that is not the only singular feature which
marked this unprecedented act.

On the one hand, it is clear from the text that John Paul
II's Act of Entrustment of the Third Millennium to Mary
Most Holy, as it is entitled, was made in virtue of her role
in God's plan as Mother of Jesus "your beloved Son the
Word of God made flesh in your womb" in whom "salva-
tion lies fully and uniquely", and that as such it does not
mention Fatima or any other approved apparition of Our
Lady. But on the other hand, in carrying out the act John
Paul II chose to associate with it, Mary as manifest in her
cult at Fatima and symbolised by the presence of the well-

known image from the shrine. For at the Holy Father's request, the image of the Virgin of Fatima had been flown over specially for the Mass of the Bishops' Jubilee on Sunday 8th October, where it was prominently placed at the foot of the large crucifix next to the altar in St Peter's Square. Thereby it recalled the scene of Our Lord on the cross recorded in John 19: 26: "When Jesus saw his mother, and the disciple whom he loved, standing near".

In my *Message of Fatima* (CTS, 1998), I have briefly traced the increasing approval which the Popes have conferred on Our Lady's message, from the reign of Pius XII onwards, and which prepared the way for the developments in John Paul II's pontificate. By associating the Virgin of Fatima with this latest and unprecedented Act of Entrustment, and by carrying it out in the presence of the most important gathering of the world's Bishops since Vatican Council II, John Paul II thereby renewed his approval of the message of Fatima in a manner which drew attention to it in a prominent fashion, but at the same time did not impose it.

Two further developments

The presence of the Virgin of Fatima at the Jubilee of the world's Bishops together with the Act of Entrustment, clearly mark this event as the most important of John Paul II's three acts with regard to Fatima in the Holy Year 2000. But in the course of the Holy Year, the Pope also conferred two further developments on the message of Fatima itself which as such are of more immediate significance, since each make an important new contribution to the way Our Lady's message is understood and received in the Church. These developments were, firstly John Paul II's Beatification at Fatima on 13th May of Francisco and Jacinta Marto, and secondly, the publication by the Congregation for the Doctrine of the Faith, on 26th June, of the text of the third part of the secret of Fatima and a number of related documents, together with a detailed commentary on its theological meaning by Cardinal Ratzinger.

Francisco and Jacinta

By his beatification of Francisco and Jacinta Marto, John Paul II has set another unique precedent. As will be seen in more detail in due course, their beatification only became possible following the Pope's promulgation of two quite recent decisions by the Congregation for the Causes of the Saints: firstly, in 1981, that a child could demonstrate heroic virtue; and secondly, on 28th June 1999, that a miraculous cure had been worked through their intercession. Before the two little shepherds, the previous youngest non-martyr to be raised to the honours of the altar was St Dominic Savio. Dominic Savio died as an adolescent about three weeks before his 15th birthday, and so was just over four years older than Francisco, who died as a child two months and one week before his 11th birthday. What makes the beatifi-cation of Francisco and Jacinta unique is that they are the first children ever to be beatified in the history of the Church, who died without suffering martyrdom.

In the beatification of Francisco and Jacinta Marto, we are contemplating the holiness of two of the three shepherd children, who were chosen by heaven to receive Our Lady's message, and who then put it into practise in their lives. After the most searching examination, the Church has proclaimed the example of their lives as models of holiness for all, especially young children and families, not because they were privileged to see, hear and speak with Our Lady, but because of their fidelity and commitment in fulfilling her requests. It was precisely for this latter reason, as the Holy Father said in his homily at the Mass of their beatification, that they became saints so quickly.

John Paul II's beatification of Francisco and Jacinta Marto has come at an opportune moment, perhaps most of all because in the appealing lives of the two little shep-herds, we see an example of the holiness which the Pope has said must be set as the priority of all pastoral initia-tives. In his recent Apostolic Letter, John Paul II stated that "holiness has emerged more clearly [in the Jubilee Year] as the dimension which expresses best the mystery of the Church. Holiness, a message that convinces without the need for words, is the living reflection of the face of Christ." (*Novo Millennio Ineunte*, Nos. 3, 29, 30, 7).

After holiness, the Pope called for prayer, union with Christ and love of God - virtues of which Blessed Francisco and Jacinta also showed forth inspiring examples in their lives.

Third part of Secret of Fatima

With regard to the unexpected publication of the third part of the secret of Fatima, which until then had been kept secret by all the Popes who had read it, from the moment it was first given to Blessed John XXIII, on 17th August 1959, John Paul II has said that the time seemed right to him to disclose it to the Church. Hence, we now know that this prophetic vision from heaven - intended exclusively for the Pope, and as such in itself a unique event in the history of the Church - brings further confirmation, depicted in terms of dramatic imagery, of Our Lady's call at Fatima for conversion of heart, prayer and penance.

As we will see, in his Theological Commentary on the third part of the secret, Cardinal Ratzinger has explained that a private revelation such as the message of Fatima, is accepted into the life of the Church when it "shows its credibility by leading me back to the definitive public Revelation". Thus it "can be a genuine help in understanding the Gospel and living it better at a particular moment in time"; but although it is a help which accordingly "should not be disregarded", at the same time "it is a help … which one is not obliged to use". In his subsequent commentary on the third part of the secret, Cardinal Ratzinger shows that the prophetic vision points to the urgency of penance, conversion and faith as "the correct response to this moment of history".

These three developments with regard to Fatima in the Holy Year have come in succession to the approval which John Paul II had already demonstrated through his four earlier acts in the period from 1982 to 1991, the thirteenth year of his pontificate.

John Paul II and Fatima

Firstly, on 13th May 1982 John Paul II became the first Pope to issue formal teaching on the meaning of Our Lady's message for the Church, in the homily he delivered on the occasion of his pilgrimage to Fatima. Secondly, by his act of consecration on the steps of St. Peter's Basilica in Rome, on 25th March 1984, he became the Pope who fulfilled Our Lady's request for the consecration of Russia. As I have sought to show in my book, *Fatima, Russia & Pope John Paul II*, it was this act more than anything else which brought about, peacefully from within, the cessation of the Marxist atheist persecution of the Church in the former Soviet Union. Thirdly, on 13th May 1989 he decreed that Francisco and Jacinta, had led lives of heroic virtue, and granted them the title Venerable, the first step towards their beatification and canonisation. Finally, on 13th May 1991, he made an Act of Entrustment to the Mother of God at Fatima, in which he thanked Our Lady for showing herself a "Mother of the nations by the unexpected changes which restored confidence to peoples [of Central and Eastern Europe] who were oppressed and humiliated for so long", and at the same time warned against "the danger of replacing Marxism with another form of atheism which, praising freedom, tends to destroy the roots of human and Christian morality".

Now once again the Pope has directed the attention of the Church towards Fatima, through the three significant new developments in the Holy Year 2000. Hence my intention in presenting this study is to elucidate the present status and significance of the message of Fatima in the Church, as it now stands in the light of these developments.

Huge crowds gather in the precinct in front of the basilica at Fatima.

POPE JOHN PAUL II'S ACT OF ENTRUSTMENT
OF THE THIRD MILLENNIUM TO MARY MOST HOLY,
8 OCTOBER 2000

It was a measure of the importance of the Pope's great Act of Entrustment of the Third Millennium to Mary Most Holy on Sunday 8th October, that it was made "collegially" at the end of the Jubilee Mass of the Bishops, over 1,400 of whom had made their Jubilee pilgrimage to Rome from every continent of the globe, to join in concelebrating with the Holy Father and 76 Cardinals. This was the largest and most representative single gathering of Bishops at St Peter's Basilica since the conclusion of the Second Vatican Council, thirty-five years previously.

Meanwhile, a Press Release on 12th September from the Vatican Press Office contained the following statement explaining the significance of the pilgrim visit to the Vatican of Our Lady of Fatima's image, which had been issued by the Central Committee for the Great Jubilee:

'It will set a Marian 'seal' on the whole Holy Year … the Act of Entrustment to Mary will thus have a particularly meaningful character, almost a crowning of the Great Jubilee... according to what was written in the introduction to the Holy Year 2000, which sees as a unity the Jubilee of Christ and the Jubilee of the Mother.' (No.12).

Preparations

The image of Our Lady of Fatima arrived in the Vatican on 6th October, and stayed that night in the Holy Father's private chapel. Early the next morning, it was taken to St Peter's Basilica, where it was exposed for the veneration and prayers of pilgrims. In the late after-noon on 7th October, the Bishops assembled in St Peter's Square for the recitation of the Rosary, in the presence of the image of Our Lady of Fatima, which was processed out from St Peter's Basilica. That day, as the Holy Father noted in his address, was the feast of the Holy Rosary, and also the first Saturday of the month - two devotions, as is well known, which are key elements in the message of Fatima. Indeed, having requested daily recitation of the Rosary six times in succession, in her final apparition at Fatima on 13th October 1917, Our Lady revealed "I am the Lady of the Rosary".

The Rosary began with a bishop reading a passage from the New Testament, for each mystery. Then, as Rosary groups world-wide joined in, from each of the five continents, a cardinal recited the first part of the Our Father, and a member of a family recited the first part of the ten Hail Marys. The fifth mystery was led by the surviving seer of Fatima, Sister Lucia, together with her community of the Carmelite Monastery of Coimbra, representing the continent of Europe, and connected by satellite with St Peter's Square. At the end of the Rosary, three Portuguese shepherd children laid a floral tribute at the feet of Our Lady.

In his address at the end of the Rosary, the Holy Father said that their prayer took place:

'In the light of the message of Fatima, whose content helps us to reflect on the history of the 20th century. To reinforce this spiritual perspective, we are fortunate to have in our midst the revered image of Our Lady of Fatima... This evening our prayer has spiritually united the human family around Mary, Regina Mundi.'

John Paul II's reference to Our Lady as Regina Mundi, or Queen of the World, prompts one to recall that on May 13th 1946, Pope Pius XII's legate, Cardinal Masella, crowned the statue of Our Lady of Fatima as Queen of the World. The Holy Father then went on to say:

'Trusting in her motherly care, at the end of our Eucharistic celebration tomorrow we will collegially make our Act of Entrustment to the Immaculate Heart of Mary. This evening, while meditating on the glorious mysteries of the Holy Rosary, we prepared inwardly for this act, taking the attitude of the Apostles in the Upper Room, gathered with Mary in unanimous and united prayer.' (*L'Osservatore Romano*, 11/10/2000, p. 1)

Purpose of the Act of Entrustment

With regard to the Act of Entrustment on the following day, Sunday 8th October, Archbishop Tarcisius Bertone, SDB, the secretary of the Congregation for the Doctrine of the Faith, explained that the Pope's intention was to foster "a renewal of communion of individuals with Christ and of the Church with Mary, who accompanies the Church with maternal care in the midst of difficulties with faith and with the world". The Pope wanted the ceremony to take place during the Jubilee for Bishops, the Archbishop continued, so that with Mary's help the bishops could "bring their faithful to a new profession in Christ"; and he deliberately chose to use the term "entrustment" because the ceremony was intended to recall the words of Jesus dying on the cross, when he entrusted his Mother to his disciples, and his disciples to his Mother. That indeed is apparent from the two opening paragraphs of the act:

'1. "Woman, behold your Son !" (Jn 19:26). As we near the end of this Jubilee Year, when you, O Mother, have offered us Jesus anew, the blessed fruit of your womb most pure, the Word made flesh, the world's Redeemer, we hear more clearly the sweet echo of his words entrusting us to you, making you our Mother: "Woman, behold your Son!"

When he entrusted to you the Apostle John, and with him the children of the Church and all people, Christ did not diminish but affirmed anew the role which is his alone as the Saviour of the world. You are the splendour which is no way dims the light of Christ, for you exist in him and through him. Everything in you is *fiat*: you are the Immaculate One, through you there shines the fullness of grace … The Church today … seeks refuges in your motherly protection and trustingly begs your intercession as she faces the challenges which lie hidden in the future …

3. Today we wish to entrust to you the future that awaits us, and we ask you to be with us on our way …Today as never before in the past, humanity stands at a crossroad. And once again, O Virgin Most Holy, salvation lies fully and uniquely in Jesus, your Son.

4. Therefore, O Mother, like the Apostle John, we wish to take you into our home (cf. Jn 19:27), that we may learn from you to become like your Son. "Woman, behold your sons!" …'

In the final paragraph, the Pope summed up his intention in making this entrustment to Mary:

'To you, Dawn of Salvation, we commit our journey through the new millennium, so that with you as guide, all people may know Christ, the light of the world and its only Saviour.'

The 1984 Consecration

Archbishop Bertone also explained that instead of using the term consecration, in this act the Pope had chosen to entrust or place under Mary's protection, the Church, her Bishops and all people, in order to convey the humble realization that we humans need help from God, and therefore ask Mary's intercession. Furthermore, the Pope did not need to repeat the consecration to her Immaculate Heart which Our Lady had requested at Fatima, since that had already been accomplished by his act of 25th March 1984 (cf. the arguments upholding the Pope's consecration in chapter 2, *Fatima, Russia & Pope John Paul II*, Gracewing, 3rd edition 1998). Earlier, on 26th June 2000, Archbishop Bertone had officially confirmed the Holy See's position on this question of the consecration, in the following passage taken from his Introduction to the document on the third part of the secret, *The Message of Fatima*, which was issued by his Congregation on that day:

'Sister Lucia personally confirmed that this solemn and universal act of consecration corresponded to what Our Lady wished - " ... Yes it has been done just as Our Lady asked, on 25 March 1984" - in a letter of 8th November 1989. *Hence any further discussion or request is without basis*' (emphasis added).

Contemplation of Mary

Finally, on 9th October, the day after the Act of Entrustment had been carried out, Cardinal Angelo Sodano went to St Damaso's patio in the Vatican, to say farewell to the pilgrim Virgin of Fatima. On behalf of the Holy Father and all his collaborators in the Holy See, the Vatican Secretary of State made a touching acknowledgment of Our Lady's visitation and profession of faith in her message:

'Holy Virgin, your venerated image returns to your beautiful shrine of Fatima. We have welcomed it with profound feelings of love, thinking of you, who once again have wanted to say to the Holy Father, John Paul II, and to all of us, his collaborators, that you take care of this house with love, the house of Peter's successor. All of us, O Mary, want to live the message you left us, when you appeared to the three little shepherds in Cova da Iria, committing ourselves to interior renewal in fidelity to our vocation.' (*Zenit*, 9/10/00)

In the last paragraph of his Act of Entrustment, John Paul II addressed Our Lady as our "Dawn of Salvation" and "guide". At the conclusion of his recent Apostolic Letter, the Pope echoed that reference when he wrote:

'During this year I have often invoked her as the "Star of the New Evangelization". Now I point to Mary once

again as the radiant dawn and sure guide for our steps …
Together, we must all imitate the contemplation of Mary,
who returned home to Nazareth from her pilgrimage to
the Holy City of Jerusalem, treasuring in her heart the
mystery of her Son (cf. Lk 2:51).' (*Novo Millennio
Ineunte*, Nos. 58, 59)

THE PUBLICATION OF THE THIRD PART OF THE SECRET

At the conclusion of the Mass for the Beatification of Francisco and Jacinta Marto, celebrated by the Holy Father at Fatima on 13th May 2000, the Vatican Secretary of State, Cardinal Sodano, stated that he had been directed by the Holy Father to make a preliminary announcement about the third part of the secret of Fatima.

Background to the publication of the third part of the secret

It is a measure of the significance which the Pope attached to the third part of the secret of Fatima, that the text of the prophetic vision was disclosed with the full authority of the Church, together with its definitive judgment upon it.

By the direction of the Pope, its forthcoming publication was announced on 13th May by the Vatican Secretary of State, Cardinal Angelo Sodano, at the conclusion of one of the Pope's important celebrations in the course of the Holy Year which also marked a unique milestone in the history of Fatima: the Beatification of Francisco and Jacinta. The reason for its disclosure was made clear at the end of Cardinal Sodano's announcement, when he stated that the Pope had charged the Congregation for the Doctrine of the Faith with publishing the third part of the secret "after the preparation of an appropriate commentary … in order that the faithful may better receive the message of Our Lady of Fatima".

Some six weeks later, on 26th June, the Congregation, of which Cardinal Ratzinger is Prefect, published the text together with his detailed 6-page theological commentary, as well as a considerable portion of accompanying documentation. At the same time, all this material was made instantaneously available world-wide on the Vatican web site in a 21-page document entitled *The Message of Fatima*. The actual text of the secret as translated from Sister Lucia's hand-written account, is just under 300 words in length and occupied one long paragraph of 18 lines.

In all these carefully prepared measures, one sees the action of the Holy Spirit in guiding the Church through John Paul II's initiatives into a more complete understanding of Our Lady's message.

When Cardinal Sodano's statement of 13th May came to be analysed, many Fatima observers were surprised to learn that the third part of the secret did not depict any future scenario that was yet to unfold, since the Cardinal's interpretation conflicted with what quite a few had mistakenly imagined it contained, in the years from 1960 onwards, the date by when Our Lady was wrongly alleged to have said the third part of the secret should be revealed. For the prophetic vision, Cardinal Sodano stated, "concerns above all the war waged by atheist systems against the Church and Christians, and it describes the immense suffering endured by witnesses to the faith in the last century of the second millennium. It is an interminable Way of the Cross led by the Popes of the twentieth century".

In a judgment at the end of his statement, Cardinal Sodano said that "the events to which the third part of the secret of Fatima refers now seem part of the past"; and in his Theological Commentary issued some six weeks later, those words were affirmed by Cardinal Ratzinger, who further commented that "insofar as individual events are described, they belong to the past".

In his commentary, Cardinal Ratzinger recalled that the interpretation of Cardinal Sodano in his statement of 13th May, was first put personally to Sister Lucia. In reply, Sister Lucia stated that she had received the vision, but that its interpretation "belonged not to the visionary but to the Church. After reading the text, however, she said that this interpretation corresponded to what she had experienced, and that on her part she thought the interpretation correct".

In his General Audience on 17th May, the Holy Father recalled his pilgrimage to Fatima, and said that he had thought it appropriate to reveal the third part of the secret "since the time seemed right to me". In an interview after he had made the announcement, Cardinal Sodano told reporters that the Holy Father had been planning to reveal the secret for some time, and that the beatification presented him with an opportune occasion. The Cardinal added that it was also "a decision tied to the closing of the millennium, to the century just passed, a century full of suffering and tribulation".

Cardinal Sodano's Annnouncement at the end of the Mass of Beatification

'Brothers and Sisters in the Lord!

At the conclusion of this solemn celebration, I feel bound to offer our beloved Holy Father Pope John Paul II, on behalf of all present, heartfelt good wishes for his approaching 80th Birthday and to thank him for his vital pastoral ministry for the good of all God's Holy Church; we present the heartfelt wishes of the whole Church.

On this solemn occasion of his visit to Fatima, His Holiness has directed me to make an announcement to you. As you know, the purpose of his visit to Fatima has been to beatify the two "little shepherds". Nevertheless he also wishes his pilgrimage to be a renewed gesture of gratitude to Our Lady for her protection during these years of his papacy. This protection seems also to be linked to the so-called third part of the "secret" of Fatima.

That text contains a prophetic vision similar to those found in Sacred Scripture, which do not describe photographically the details of future events, but synthesize and compress against a single background facts which extend through time in an unspecified succession and duration. As a result, the text must be interpreted in a symbolic key.

The vision of Fatima concerns above all the war waged by atheistic systems against the Church and Christians, and it describes the immense suffering endured by the witnesses of the faith in the last century of the second millennium. It is an interminable Way of the Cross led by the Popes of the twentieth century.

According to the interpretation of the "little shepherds", which was also confirmed recently by Sister Lucia, "the Bishop clothed in white" who prays for all the faithful is the Pope. As he makes his way with great difficulty towards the Cross amid the corpses of those who were martyred (Bishops, priests, men and women Religious and many lay people), he too falls to the ground, apparently dead, under a hail of gunfire.

After the assassination attempt on 13th May 1981, it appeared evident that it was "a mother's hand that guided the bullet's path", enabling "the Pope in his throes" to halt "at the threshold of death" (Pope John Paul II, Meditation from the Policlinico Gemelli to the Italian Bishops, *Insegnamenti*, XVII, 1 [1994], 1061). On the occasion of a visit to Rome by the then Bishop of Leiria-Fatima, the Pope decided to give him the bullet which had remained in the jeep after the assassination attempt, so that it might be kept in the shrine. By the Bishop's decision, the bullet was later set in the crown of the statue of Our Lady of Fatima.

The successive events of 1989 led, both in the Soviet Union and in a number of countries of Eastern Europe, to the fall of the Communist regimes which promoted atheism. For this too His Holiness offers heartfelt thanks to the Most Holy Virgin. In other parts of the world, however, attacks against the Church and against Christians, with the burden of suffering they bring, tragically continue. Even if the events to which the third part of the "secret" of Fatima refers now seem part of the past, Our Lady's call to conversion and penance, issued at the start of the twentieth century, remains timely and urgent today. "The Lady of the message seems to read the signs of the times—the signs of our time—with special insight... The insistent invitation of Mary Most Holy to penance is nothing but the manifestation of her maternal concern for the fate of the human family, in need of conversion and forgiveness" (Pope John Paul II, Message for the 1997 World Day of the Sick, No. 1, *Insegnamenti*, XIX, 2 [1996], 561).

In order that the faithful may better receive the message of Our Lady of Fatima, the Pope has charged the Congregation for the Doctrine of the Faith with making public the third part of the "secret", after the preparation of an appropriate commentary.

Brothers and sisters, let us thank Our Lady of Fatima for her protection. To her maternal intercession let us entrust the Church of the Third Millennium.

Sub tuum praesidium confugimus, Sancta Dei Genetrix! Intercede pro Ecclesia. Intercede pro Papa nostro Ioanne Paulo II. Amen. (Fatima, 13 May 2000).'

The decision to publish the third part of the secret

Cardinal Sodano's statement on 13th May certainly caused a stir in the Church. But as it was only a partial disclosure summarising the content of the secret, it did not detract from the importance of the Beatification. Instead, it created a sense of expectancy, by focussing attention on the forthcoming publication of the text later in the summer, which the Holy Father had charged the Congregation for the Doctrine of the Faith to undertake, together with a commentary.

Looking back, it can be seen that the decision to reveal the secret in two stages, succeeded in making it known without causing it to overshadow either the Beatification or the Act of Entrustment which was to follow on 8th October.

When viewed in the context of the events taking place in the Holy Year, it was in fact an appropriate moment at which to speak of the third part of the secret. For in his homily at the Mass of Beatification, the Holy Father reminded people that six days previously, on Sunday 7th May, he had led an impressive ecumenical ceremony at the Colosseum in Rome, to commemorate "the many witnesses to the faith in the 20th century, recalling the tribulations they suffered... Here in Fatima these times of tribulation were foretold and Our Lady asked for prayer and penance to shorten them".

The sufferings foretold by Our Lady also touched the Holy Father, and were the subject of two visions experienced by Jacinta, as recorded by Sister Lucia in her third memoir, and acknowledged by John Paul II in his homily at the Mass of Beatification: "I also express my gratitude to Blessed Jacinta for the sacrifices and prayers offered for the Holy Father, whom she saw suffering greatly".

The Holy Father himself had personally experienced the period of intense persecution and suffering of his countrymen in Poland, which began in the Second World War under the Nazis, and continued after the war under Communist rule, until the advent of President Mikhail Gorbachev. It was while Karol Wojtyla was attending the secret seminary which Archbishop Sapieha had organised in the bishop's palace at Krakow, that Sister Lucia wrote down the third part of the secret in obedience to the order of her bishop, on 3rd January 1944. Just over one year later, on 17th January 1945, the German forces of occupation withdrew from the city in the face of the advancing Red Army, and as the Soviet Union extended its grip over Poland and other Eastern European countries, it proceeded to instal the rule of atheistic Communism. Thus there commenced the period of war, persecution, suffering and martyrdom for the Church, as foretold by Our Lady in the second part of the secret that she had confided to the three little shepherds on 13th July 1917.

Prior to its publication by John Paul II, even though the text of the third part of the secret had never been revealed, nevertheless some purely speculative theories as to its probable content, lacking any solid foundation, would reappear in print from time to time. Some of these theories indeed were so far-fetched that they reflected adversely on the credibility of the message of Fatima as a whole, which had long been accepted and made known by the Church, and increasingly approved by the Popes.

John Paul II's decision to publish the third part of the secret, in the context of a fully comprehensive account, together with a definitive commentary by Cardinal Ratzinger, brought an immediate benefit to the message of Fatima, by ending the controversy which had inevitably swirled round that part of the secret which until then had remained unknown.

The beatification provided an opportune moment at which to announce the forthcoming publication of a prophetic vision which may be seen from its content to form a logical continuation of the two previous parts; and the consistent reference of Cardinal Sodano and Cardinal Ratzinger to "the third part of the secret", emphasises the fact that it is one single secret divided into three parts, all of which were revealed in continuous succession in the apparition of 13th July.

On the occasion of his first pilgrimage to Fatima, Sister Lucia sent a letter on the third part of the secret to the Holy Father, dated 12th May 1982. In this letter, which was published as part of the accompanying documentation, Sister Lucia showed that the third part of the secret refers to the second part:

'The third part of the secret refers to Our Lady's words [in the second part of the secret]: 'If not [Russia] will spread her errors throughout the world, causing wars and persecutions of the Church. The good will be martyred; the Holy Father will have much to suffer; various nations will be annihilated' (13-VII-1917). The third part of the secret is a symbolic revelation, referring to this part of the Message, conditioned by whether we accept or not what the Message itself asks of us: 'If my requests are heeded, Russia will be converted, and there will be peace; if not, she will spread her errors throughout the world, etc'.

Since we did not heed this appeal of the Message, we see that it has been fulfilled, Russia has invaded the world with her errors…'

The text of the third part of the secret of Fatima

'I write in obedience to you, my God, who command me to do so through his Excellency the Bishop of Leiria and through your Most Holy Mother and mine.

After the two parts which I have already explained, at the left of Our Lady and a little above, we saw an Angel with a flaming sword in his left hand; flashing, it gave out flames that looked as though they would set the world on fire; but they died out in contact with the splendour that Our Lady radiated towards him from her right hand: pointing to the earth with his right hand, the Angel cried out in a loud voice: 'Penance, Penance, Penance!'. And we saw in an immense light that is God: 'something similar to how people appear in a mirror when they pass in front of it' a Bishop dressed in

White 'we had the impression that it was the Holy Father'. Other Bishops, Priests, men and women Religious were going up a steep mountain, at the top of which there was a big Cross of rough-hewn trunks as of a cork-tree with the bark; before reaching there the Holy Father passed through a big city half in ruins and half trembling with halting step, afflicted with pain and sorrow, he prayed for the souls of the corpses he met on his way; having reached the top of the mountain, on his knees at the foot of the big Cross he was killed by a group of soldiers who fired bullets and arrows at him, and in the same way there died one after another the other Bishops, Priests, men and women Religious, and various lay people of different ranks and positions. Beneath the two arms of the Cross there were two Angels each with a crystal aspersorium in his hand, in which they gathered up the blood of the Martyrs and with it sprinkled the souls that were making their way to God. (Tuy-3-1-1944).'

The content of *The Message of Fatima*

In his 4-page Introduction to the above document, Archbishop Tarcisius Bertone, SDB, secretary to the Congregation for the Doctrine of the Faith, relates that the third part of the secret was placed in the Secret Archives of the Holy Office on 4th April 1957. It was first seen but not opened by Pope John XXIII, on 17th August 1959. Note 1 contains a photostat of John XXIII's hand-written entry in his diary for that date, recording that Fr. Pierre Paul

Philippe OP of the Holy Office, with the agreement of
Cardinal Alfredo Ottaviani, brought him the envelope con-
taining the secret. Thereafter, Pope Paul VI read the con-
tents on 27th March 1965, and decided not to publish it; and
Pope John Paul II read it while he was convalescing, some
weeks after the assassination attempt on 13th May 1981.

Archbishop Bertone then cites the major part of John
Paul II's act of consecration of 25th March 1984, and the
text of Sister Lucia's letter to the Holy Father dated 12th
May 1982, from which we have quoted above.

The next two pages contain photostats of Sister Lucia's
original manuscripts of the first and second parts of the
secret, taken from her third memoir of 31st August 1941,
followed by their translation. These are followed by further
photostats and then the translation of the third part of the
secret. After that comes a photostat together with the translation of the Holy Father's letter to Sister Lucia dated 19th
April 2000, in which he asked her to receive Archbishop
Bertone, who "will come in my name and ask certain ques-
tions about the interpretation of the third part of the secret".

In the report of that meeting, which took place on 27th
April 2000, Sister Lucia confirmed that the principal figure in the vision was the Pope. She continued: "Our Lady
did not tell us the name of the Pope … but it was the
Pope who was suffering and that made us suffer too". She
fully agreed with the Pope's claim, that "it was a mother's hand that guided the bullet's path and in his throes

the Pope halted at the threshold of death". Sister Lucia
also said that it was herself, not Our Lady, who had fixed
1960 as the date after which the secret could be revealed.
"I wrote down what I saw; however, it was not for me to
interpret it, but for the Pope".

At this point, one was astonished and pleased to learn
that notwithstanding her advanced years, Sister Lucia has
prepared a new manuscript, written by way of replying to
the many letters she continues to receive from Marian
devotees and pilgrims. The work "gathers together in the
style of catechesis and exhortation, thoughts and reflec-
tions which express Sister Lucia's feelings and her clear
and unaffected spirituality".

Lucia, Francisco and Jacinta in 1917. By kind permision of Dr Luciano Coelho Cristino, Archivist of the Fatima Sanctuary.

CARDINAL RATZINGER'S THEOLOGICAL COMMENTARY ON THE THIRD PART OF THE SECRET

The theological status of Public Revelation and private revelations

In the first part of his commentary, Cardinal Ratzinger sets out "some basic clarification of the way in which, according to Church teaching, phenomena such as Fatima are to be under-stood within the life of faith". The Cardinal begins by citing the passage from St John of the Cross in the *Catechism of the Catholic Church* (No. 65), which explains the finality and completeness of the public Revelation God has made of himself in Christ: "In giving us his Son, his only Word (for he possesses no other), he spoke everything at once to us in this sole Word - and he has no more to say".

However, while "the Church is tied to this unique event of sacred history and to the word of the Bible, which guarantees and interprets it", Cardinal Ratzinger continues, "this does not mean that the Church can now look only to the past, and that she is condemned to sterile repetition". Citing the *Catechism of the Catholic Church*, the Cardinal says that "even if Revelation is already com-plete, it has not been made completely explicit; it remains for Christian faith gradually to grasp its full significance over the course of the centuries" (No. 66).

This gradual development is the work of the Holy Spirit, and Cardinal Ratzinger then cites the three essential ways defined by the Second Vatican Council, "in which the Spirit guides in the Church" and causes the word to grow: "through the meditation and study of the faithful, through the deep understanding which comes from spiritual experience, and through the preaching of 'those who, in the succession of the episcopate, have received the sure charism of truth'" (*Dei Verbum*, No. 8).

It is in this context, says Cardinal Ratzinger, that we can now "understand rightly the concept of 'private revelation', which refers to all the visions and revelations which have taken place since the completion of the New Testament". He then cites from the *Catechism of the Catholic Church*, the following criterion for accepting those private revelations "some of which have been recognised by the authority of the Church ... It is not their role to improve or complete Christ's definitive Revelation, but to help live more fully by it in a certain period of history" (No. 67).

This clarifies two points. Firstly, the definitive public Revelation "demands faith ... in God and in his word (which) is different from any other human faith, trust or opinion. The certainty that it is God who is speaking gives me the assurance that I am in touch with truth itself". Secondly, "private revelation is a help to this faith, and shows its credibility precisely by leading me back to the definitive public Revelation".

Cardinal Ratzinger then shows the two ways by which a recognised private revelation can be accepted. Firstly, in the words of the classic definition of Cardinal Prospero Lambertini, the future Pope Benedict XIV: "An assent of Catholic faith is not due to revelations approved in this way … (but) rather an assent of human faith in keeping with the requirements of prudence, which puts them before us as probable and credible to piety". Secondly, Cardinal Ratzinger sets out three elements governing ecclesiastical approval of a private revelation, from the work of the eminent Flemish scholar, E. Dhanis, and which he describes as follows:

'the message contains nothing contrary to faith or morals; it is lawful to make it public; and the faithful are authorised to accept it with prudence.'

Summing up the position, Cardinal Ratzinger says:

'Such a message can be a genuine help in understanding the Gospel and living it better at a particular moment in time; therefore it should not be disregarded. It is a help which is offered, but which one is not obliged to use. The criterion for the truth and value of a private revelation is therefore its orientation to Christ himself. When it leads us away from him … or even presents itself as another and better plan of salvation, more important than the

Gospel, then it certainly does not come from the Holy Spirit, who guides us more deeply into the Gospel and not away from it.'

Finally, Cardinal Ratzinger asks how private revelations can be classified correctly in relation to Scripture. Quoting St. Paul's admonition to the Thessalonians, not to quench the Spirit nor despise prophecy, but to test everything and hold fast to what is good (I: 5:19-21), the Cardinal goes on to say:

'In every age the Church has received the charism of prophecy, which must be scrutinised but not scorned. On this point it should be kept in mind that prophecy in the biblical sense does not mean to predict the future but to explain the will of God for the present, and therefore show the right path to take for the future ...

The prophetic word is a warning or a consolation, or both together. In this sense there is a link between the charism of prophecy and the category of the 'signs of the times', which Vatican II brought to light anew ... to interpret the signs of the times in the light of faith means to recognise the presence of Christ in every age. In the private revelations approved by the Church - and therefore also in Fatima - this is the point: they help us to understand the signs of the times and to respond to them rightly in faith.'

Cardinal Ratzinger's Interpretation of the Third Part of the Secret

We will now pass over Cardinal Ratzinger's observations on the anthropological structure of private revelations, which do not relate to the present study, and proceed to summarise his interpretation of the third part of the secret, at the conclusion of his Theological Commentary.

The way to Salvation

In order "to save souls", which the Cardinal describes as the key word of the first and second parts of the secret, the children were shown the fall of "the souls of poor sinners", in the fearful vision of hell. They were exposed to this moment

"'in order to save souls' - to show the way to salvation …To reach this goal, the way indicated …is devotion to the Immaculate Heart of Mary... In biblical language, the "heart" indicates the centre of human life, the point where reason, will, temperament and sensitivity converge, where the person finds his unity and interior orientation. According to Matthew 5:8, the "immaculate heart" is a heart which, with God's grace, has come to perfect interior unity and therefore "sees God". To be "devoted" to the Immaculate Heart of Mary means therefore to embrace this attitude of heart which makes the *fiat* -"your will be done" - the defining centre of one's whole life … From whom might we better learn in every age than from the Mother of the Lord ? ...

"To save souls" has emerged as the key word of the first and second parts of the "secret", and the key word of this third part is the threefold cry, "Penance, Penance, Penance!" The beginning of the Gospel comes to mind: "Repent and believe in the Good News" (Mk. 1:15). To understand the signs of the times means to accept the urgency of penance - of conversion - of faith. This is the correct response to this moment of history, characterised by the grave perils outlined in the images that follow.'

It is man himself who "has forged the flaming sword" representing "the threat of judgment which looms over the world". Opposed to this stands

'the splendour of the Mother of God and, stemming from this in a certain way, the summons to penance. In this way, the importance of human freedom is underlined: the future is not unchangeably set, and the image which the children saw is in no way a film preview of a future in which nothing can be changed. Indeed, the whole point of the vision is to bring freedom onto the scene and to steer freedom in a positive direction... to mobilise the forces of change in the right direction. Therefore we must totally discount fatalistic explanations of the secret ...Rather, the vision speaks of dangers and how we might be saved from them.'

The symbols: mountain, city, cross

Cardinal Ratzinger then makes a detailed analysis of the three symbolic places of the action: a steep mountain, a great city in ruins and a large rough-hewn cross. He comments:

'In the vision we can recognize the last century as a century of martyrs, a century of suffering and persecution for the Church, a century of World Wars and the many local wars which filled the last fifty years ...

In the *Via Crucis* of an entire century, the figure of the Pope has a special role ... Beginning from Pius X up to the present Pope, they all shared the sufferings of the century and strove to go forward through all the anguish along the path which leads to the Cross. In the vision, the Pope too is killed along with the martyrs.

When, after the attempted assassination on 13th May 1981, the Holy Father had the text of the third part of the "secret" brought to him, was it not inevitable that he should see in it his own fate ? ... That here a "mother's hand" had deflected the fateful bullet only shows once more that there is no immutable destiny, that faith and prayer are forces which can influence history, and that in the end prayer is more powerful than bullets and faith more powerful than armies ...

Beneath the arms of the cross ... the blood of Christ and the blood of the martyrs are considered as one ... the death of the witnesses is fruitful for the future life of the Church. Therefore the vision of the third part of the secret, so distressing at first, concludes with an image of hope: no suffering is in vain…'

The meaning of the secret as a whole, what it says to us, is: "the exhortation to prayer as the path of 'salvation for souls' and likewise, the summons to penance and conversion".

Overcome the world

In his final paragraph, Cardinal Ratzinger makes the following comment on the meaning of the justly famous phrase, "my Immaculate Heart will triumph":

'The Heart open to God, purified by contemplation of God, is stronger than guns and weapons of every kind. The *fiat* of Mary, the word of her heart, has changed the history of the world, because …thanks to her *Yes*, God could become man in our world and remains so for all time.

The Evil One has power in the world … because our human freedom continually lets itself be led away from God. But since God himself took a human heart and has thus steered human freedom towards what is good, the freedom to choose evil no longer has the last word. From that time forth, the word that prevails is this: "In this world you will have tribulation, but take heart, I have overcome the world" (Jn 16:33). The message of Fatima invites us to trust in this promise.'

The message of Fatima, Pope John Paul II's teaching and the Theological Commentary

All who seek to follow Our Lady's message in fidelity to the teaching of the Church will welcome the Holy Father's decision, not simply to reveal the third part of the secret, but in doing so, to make it known with the full authority and explanatory interpretation of the Church's Magisterium, and in the context of a considerable body of supporting documentation. Underlining the Holy See's view, that "Our Lady's call to conversion and penance … remains timely and urgent today", as he stated in his announcement on 13th May 2000, Cardinal Sodano went on to explain that, at the direction of the Holy Father, the third part of the secret was going to be made public, "in order that the faithful may better receive the message of Our Lady of Fatima … after the preparation of an appropriate commentary".

As we have seen, the Holy Father's mandate was duly fulfilled by Cardinal Ratzinger when he published the content of the prophetic vision together with his detailed Theological Commentary, on 26th June. In his Commentary, Cardinal Ratzinger has expressed the authoritative judgment of the Magisterium, and provided us with the correct basis for understanding the way in which the private revelation of Our Lady's message at Fatima is accepted by the Church, and how the "secret" is to be interpreted.

Conversion and Repentance

The Cardinal's subsequent interpretation then leads one to the spiritual focal point and meaning of the whole of the secret, which had now been fully revealed in its entirety for the first time. As Cardinal Ratzinger says, while the key word of the first and second parts of the secret is "to save souls", it is the threefold cry of the Angel: "Penance, Penance, Penance !" which is the key word of the third part.

In these two key words, it is evident that the secret as a whole reiterates in an amplified form the theme at the heart of the message for which the Angel of Peace came to prepare the seers at the very outset of the apparitions. For in his second apparition in the summer of 1916, the Angel instructed the three little shepherds: "Pray! Pray very much! ... Make of everything you can a sacrifice, and offer it to God as an act of reparation for the sins by which He is offended and in supplication for the conversion of sinners".

"These words were indelibly impressed upon our minds", Sister Lucia recorded in her Fourth Memoir. "They were like a light which made us understand who God is, how He loves us and desires to be loved, the value of sacrifice, how pleasing it is to him and how, on account of it, He grants the grace of conversion to sinners. It was for this reason that we began, from then on, to offer to the Lord all that mortified us ..."

In the course of his homily at Fatima on 13th May 1982, John Paul II defined conversion and repentance as the two main reasons why the Church has accepted the message of Fatima. In the first formal teaching to be pronounced on the message by a reigning Pope, John Paul II stated:

'If the Church has accepted the message of Fatima, it is above all because that message contains a truth and a call whose basic content is the truth and the call of the Gospel itself. "Repent and believe in the Gospel" (Mk 1:15). These are the first words that the Messiah addressed to humanity. The message of Fatima is, in its basic nucleus, a call to conversion and repentance, as in the Gospel.'

In his homily at the Beatification of Francisco and Jacinta, on 13th May 2000, this is how the Holy Father explained the reason for Our Lady's apparitions:

'In her motherly concern, the Blessed Virgin came here to Fatima to ask men and women "to stop offending God, Our Lord, who is already very offended". It is a mother's sorrow that compels her to speak; the destiny of her children is at stake. For this reason she asks the little shepherds: "Pray, pray very much and make sacrifices for sinners; many souls go to hell because they have no one to pray and make sacrifices for them".'

In passing, let us note that in the course of his General Audience of 28th July 1989, the Holy Father spoke about hell, and taught that the images in the New Testament of the place destined for evildoers

'Show the complete frustration and emptiness of life without God. Rather than a place, hell indicates the state of those who freely and definitively separate themselves from God, the source of all life and joy …

"Eternal damnation", therefore, is not attributed to God's initiative, because in his merciful love he can only desire the salvation of the beings he created. In reality it is the creature who closes himself or herself to God's love. "Damnation" consists precisely in definitive separation from God, freely chosen by the human person and confirmed by death that seals this choice for ever. God's judgment ratifies this state.' (cited in *The Spirituality of the Little Shepherds*, p. 59)

At the end of his announcement, after the Mass of Beatification, Cardinal Sodano cited a further pronouncement by John Paul II on Fatima, from his Message for the 1997 World Day of the Sick:

'The Lady of the message seems to read the signs of the times - the signs of our times - with special insight … The insistent invitation of Mary Most Holy to penance is nothing but the manifestation of her maternal concern for the fate of the human family, in need of conversion and forgiveness. '

With regard to penance, in his Apostolic Letter on Suffering, John Paul II taught that:

'The purpose of penance is to overcome evil, which under different forms lies dormant in man. Its purpose is also to strengthen goodness both in man himself and in his relationships with others and especially with God (*Salvifici Doloris*, No. 13).'

Finally, in his General Audience of 17th May 2000, on his return to Rome after carrying out the Beatification of Francisco and Jacinta, the Holy Father said:

'A message of conversion and hope has spread from Fatima throughout the world … It invites believers … to do penance so that hearts may be opened to conversion. This is the true Gospel of Christ, which is presented anew to our generation particularly tried by events of the past. God's appeal to us through the Blessed Virgin still retains all its timeliness today.'

Affirming the Gospel

Since the apparitions were approved in 1930, each Pope "has referred to Fatima in various ways, but always as a reaffirmation of the Gospel", as the American authority on Fatima, Fr. Robert Fox, has stated (*Documents of Fatima*, Fatima Family Apostolate, 1992, p. xvi). In fact, as was emphasised by the past Bishop of Leiria-Fatima, Alberto Cosme do Amaral, who welcomed Pope John Paul II to the shrine in 1982 and 1991, Fatima brings one into living contact with the Gospel. In his Prologue to Fr. Fernando Leite's biography, *Francisco of Fatima* (English edition, Sept. 1999, p. 5), Bishop Amaral stated: "to know the message is to know the Gospel, to live the message is to live the Gospel. To accept the message is to accept Revelation as interpreted by the authentic Magisterium of the Church. There is almost no article of the Faith of the Church which is not reaffirmed, explicitly or implicitly, in the message of Fatima, understanding this in its widest and deepest sense".

Thus in these pronouncements we see that the message of Fatima is oriented to Christ and the Gospel, and so fulfils the fundamental criterion for the truth and value of a private revelation, as set down by Cardinal Ratzinger in his Theological Commentary.

Reading the signs of the times

Thereafter, it is evident on the one hand, that the Pope cannot and has not sought to impose the message of Fatima, since as a private revelation, in the words of Cardinal Ratzinger, "it is a help which is offered, but which one is not obliged to use". But on the other hand, it is also clear that by his acts, his teaching and his personal example, John Paul II has sought to show the Church that

Our Lady's message has a significant value as "a genuine help in understanding the Gospel and living it better" at the present moment in time, because "the Lady of the message seems to read the signs of the times - the signs of our time - with special insight", as he said, in the passage above cited by Cardinal Sodano.

John Paul II explained the significance of Fatima as a sign of the times, in a message to the Bishop of Fatima dated 1st October 1997, to commemorate "the 80th anniversary of that 13th October 1917, when the miraculous 'dance of the sun' occurred in the sky…

'On the threshold of the third millennium, as we observe the signs of the times in this 20th century, Fatima is certainly one of the greatest, among other reasons because its message announces many of the later events and conditions them on the response to its appeals: signs such as the two world wars, but also great gatherings of nations and people marked by dialogue and peace; the oppression and turmoil suffered by various nations and peoples, but also the voice and opportunities given to peoples and individuals who in the meantime have emerged on the international scene; the crises, desertions and many sufferings of the Church's members, but also a renewed and intense feeling of solidarity and mutual dependence in Christ's Mystical Body, which is being strengthened in all the baptized, in accor-

dance with their vocation and mission; the separation
from and abandonment of God by individuals and soci-
eties, but also the in-breaking of the Spirit of Truth in
hearts and communities to the point of sacrifice and
martyrdom to save "God's image and likeness in man"
(Gn 1:27), to save man from himself.

Among these and other signs of the times, as I said,
Fatima stands out, and helps us to see the hand of God,
our providential Guide and patient and compassionate
Father also in the 20th century.

In analysing the human separation from God in the
light of Fatima, we should recall that it is not the first
time that, feeling rejected and despised by man but
respecting his freedom, God allows man to feel distant
from him, with the consequent obscuring of life, which
causes darkness to fall on history, but afterwards provides
a refuge. This already happened on Calvary... and what
did Christ do? After invoking the mercy of God (Lk
23:34), he entrusted humanity to Mary, his Mother:
"Woman, behold your son" (Jn 19:26).'

Summary

To sum up the status of the message of Fatima in the
Church today, because Our Lady's appeal comes to us
through a private revelation, we are not obliged to use
this help. However, that does not mean it should be disregarded. Indeed, if we want to show our love for Christ

and His Church, and our desire to do His Will, then ought we not first of all to ask ourselves why in the course of his pontificate, Pope John Paul II has repeatedly sought to draw the attention of the Church to the importance of Our Lady's message, as a "genuine help in understanding the Gospel and living it better" at this critical moment in time, when "as never before in the past, humanity stands at a crossroads".

Next, we should also consider, as Cardinal Ratzinger has shown, how the vision of the Mother of God in splendour in the third part of the secret - "the power which stands opposed to the force of destruction" - underlines our freedom to work to overcome the evil which man has brought on himself by sin, by responding to her call for prayer and penance, so that souls may be saved and sinners converted, so that "the darkness will not prevail over the light" (Act of Entrustment, 8th Oct. 2000). Thus we need to be aware that by the way we exercise our freedom to respond, or not to respond, to the Holy Virgin's call, we have the power to alter the course of future events. For the message of Fatima "announces many of the later events *and conditions them on the response to its appeals*" (my emphasis) , as John Paul II stated, in his message dated 1st October 1997 cited above; and this means, as Cardinal Ratzinger stated, "that faith and prayer are forces which can influence history, and that in the end, prayer is more powerful than bullets and faith more powerful than armies".

Finally, as we will see in the next part of this study, it was because they freely responded to the appeal of Mary Most Holy that Blessed Francisco and Jacinta Marto became assiduous in the practice of prayer and penance, and were raised up to the height of Christian perfection that has now been formally recognised by their Beatification. Hence the Church has now placed before us, as models to imitate on this path of sanctification, the appealing example of the lives of two shepherd children "through whom the Mother of Christ recommended to the entire Church persevering prayer, conversion of heart and penance as irreplaceable means of holiness and instruments of perfection", as was proclaimed in the Decree on the Miracle issued by the Congregation for the Causes of Saints on 28th June 1999.

Thus the prophetic message of Fatima, which the little shepherds showed forth in their lives, in the words of Cardinal Ratzinger, "does not mean to predict the future but to explain the will of God for the present, and therefore show the right path to take for the future ... To understand the signs of the times means to accept the urgency of penance - of conversion - of faith. This is the correct response to this moment of history".

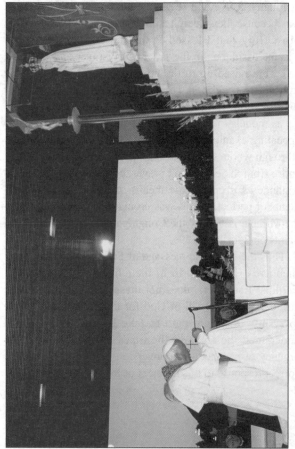

John Paul prays in front of the statue of Our Lady of Fatima, 13th May 2000.

THE BEATIFICATION OF
FRANCISCO & JACINTA MARTO

Beatification Ceremony on 13 May 2000

After arriving in Fatima on the evening of 12th May, the beloved figure of the indefatigable Pope John Paul II was greeted with rapturous applause as he made his way through the huge crowd of over 600,000 faithful to the *Capelinha*, the Little Chapel of the Apparitions. Then, at a word, the whole gathering fell silent, as the Holy Father knelt in prayer at the feet of the famous statue, which stands at the exact height on the precise spot where the Holy Virgin had first appeared to the little shepherds eighty-three years ago. When he rose, the Holy Father placed at the foot of the statue, the gift of one of his most precious possessions, the gold ring which had been given to him after his election as Pope in October 1978, by the late Primate of Poland, Cardinal Stefan Wyszynski of Warsaw. As he stated in his General Audience five days later, on 17th May, with this gift he wanted to renew symbolically his thanks to Mary "for what she wished to communicate to the Church through these children, and for the protection she has given me throughout my Pontificate".

On Saturday 13th, the Holy Father first met briefly with Sister Lucia, before concelebrating Mass with four cardinals and ten bishops of his entourage, together with all the bishops of Portugal, other cardinals and bishops from various parts of the world, and nearly one thousand priests. After the introductory rites, in response to the petition of the Bishop of Fatima, the Pope then proclaimed that Francisco and Jacinta "may be called Blessed and may have their feast celebrated each year, locally according to the norms of the privilege, on 20th February". The readings of the liturgy - Rev. 11: 19a, 12:1, 3-6a, 17; Col 1: 24-28; Mt 11: 25 - "were specially chosen to reflect the lives of the seers and the message of Fatima", noted *L'Osservatore Romano* of 17th May. The Pope gave Holy Communion to Sister Lucia, to Emilia Santos, whose miraculous cure in 1989 had paved the way for the beatification, to a group of Portuguese children, and to a number of other persons.

When the Holy Father had read out the Rite of Beatification, there was loud applause in the square, and a newly-composed hymn to the Little Shepherds was sung, with a touching refrain invoking "Francisco and Jacinta, pray for us !" At the same moment, two huge and well known black and white pictures of the newly-proclaimed Blesseds were uncovered, clearly visible from the far end of the vast square. They had been hung on either side of the statue of the Immaculate Heart of Mary located in the centre of the basilica façade, and were slowly exposed to view as the flag of Portugal that had been covering Francisco on the left of the statue, and the papal banner of white and gold covering Jacinta on the right, were gradually wound down into a cylinder.

Sister Lucia looked radiant, and must have rejoiced that in her 93rd year God had preserved her to witness the honours of the altar being conferred upon her dearly loved childhood companions, in the very place where she had been privileged to converse with the Holy Mother of God.

It is thanks to Sister Lucia's remarkable powers of memory and vivid description, that we have been given so many precious insights into the seers' lives at the time of Our Lady's apparitions. In her Fifth Memoir, which was only recently published in English in April 1999, she writes movingly that her father never lost confidence in the protection of Our Lady, despite losing the income from his fields in the Cova da Iria as a result of the apparitions. In fact, he donated the site for the Capelinha as well as the land to provide access to it (*Fatima in Lucia's Own Words*, vol. II, April 1999, pp. 29, 34).

So now, all those years later, and probably for the last time, Sister Lucia stood once more in the Cova da Iria that had been made sacred by the presence of Our Lady. But this time she looked out on a scene so unimaginably different from that of her childhood memories: the moving spectacle of a vast assembly of people from all over the world, at least six hundred thousand strong, gathered in peace, joy and communion of faith in the vast natural amphitheatre of the Cova da Iria - the "hollow of peace". They had come to join with the Holy Father in giving praise and thanks to God for the rite that would raise her beloved childhood companions to the highest honours of the altar except for canonisation. In evocative words, the Holy Father proclaimed in his homily that "with this rite, the Church wishes to put on the candelabrum these two candles which God lit to illumine humanity in its dark and anxious hours".

What the Church intends by Beatification and Canonisation

The author is indebted to Fr. Louis Kondor, SVD, Vice-Postulator of the Causes of Canonisation of Francisco and Jacinta Marto, for permission to reproduce the information in this section, most of which has been taken from The *Seers of Fatima*, the bulletin which is published by the office of his Postulation Centre in Fatima. This quarterly publication, usually four pages in length, is sent to those who enrol in the League of Prayer and Sacrifice to promote the Causes of the Canonisation of Francisco and Jacinta Marto, which Fr. Kondor founded in 1963.

The process for the Causes of the Canonisation of Francisco and Jacinta Marto of Fatima was formally introduced in 1952, and its preliminary work was concluded in 1979. In his bulletin, Fr. Kondor has admitted that the path leading to the beatification had not been easy, and that "the first step required was for the process to be accepted". The problem was that Francisco and Jacinta are the first children in the history of the Church to be considered for canonisation, who died not as martyrs but as confessors. Jacinta was born on 11th March 1910, and died on 20th February 1920, just over two weeks before her 10th birthday. Francisco was born on 11th June 1908, and died on 4th April 1919, two months and one week before his 11th birthday.

The possibility of finding true *martyrs* among children and adolescents has always been recognised by the Church, as Archbishop Saraiva Martins, Prefect of the Congregation for the Causes of Saints, pointed out in an interview in Rome on 13th July 1999. Archbishop Martins cited the examples of St Agnes and St Maria Goretti, both aged 12 and who were martyred in the third and twentieth centuries respectively, as well as the fifteen children between the ages of 10 and 13 years old among the Japanese martyrs who died between 1617 and 1632 and were beatified in 1867.

"However, between 1588, when the dicastery for the Causes of Saints was instituted, and 1981, it seems that the youngest saint who is not a martyr was St Dominic Savio", stated Archbishop Martins. St. Dominic Savio had died in adolescence, about three weeks before his 15th birthday. On 2nd April 1981, a Plenary Assembly of the

Congregation for the Causes of Saints was held, and after prolonged discussion it was decided that even though children as young as Francisco and Jacinta had not suffered martyrdom, they could have practiced virtue to a heroic degree, and so be fitting subjects for canonisation. The Holy Father ratified that decision, and it then became possible to proceed with their Causes of Canonisation.

The Decree of the heroic Virtues of Francisco and Jacinta Marto

The first step in that process was to submit their lives, their writings and their reputation for virtue to a meticulously thorough examination by the most experienced experts . They came through that test with the highest distinction when, on 13th May 1989, the Holy Father promulgated a decree that the servants of God "practised to an heroic degree the theological virtues of Faith, Hope and Charity towards God and towards neighbour, and also the cardinal virtues of Prudence, Justice, Temperance and Fortitude and their associates", and granted them the title Venerable.

The decree was published in full by Fr. Kondor in the issue of The *Seers of Fatima* for May/August 1989, and consists of some three pages for each child. We cite the following extracts, beginning with the Decree on Jacinta.

"'Unless you change and become like little children you will never enter the kingdom of heaven" (Mt 18: 3). With these words "Jesus exalted the active role that little ones have in the Kingdom of God. They are the eloquent symbol and exalted image of those moral and spiritual conditions that are essential for entering into the Kingdom of God and for living the logic of total confidence in the Lord"… (*Christifideles Laici*, 47).

Endowed with a lively, expansive and joyful disposition, she loved to play and dance; she captured the sympathy of others, although she… disliked being contradicted so much that she pouted easily… Afterwards, however, she changed completely and became a splendid model of humility, mortification and generosity…

She said, "I love Our Lord so much ! At times, I seem to have a fire in my heart, but it does not burn me". She dearly loved to contemplate Christ Crucified and she was moved to tears on hearing the account of the Passion… She nourished an ardent devotion to the Eucharist, which she visited frequently and for long periods in the parish Church, concealing herself in the pulpit where no one could see or distract her. She longed to receive the Body of Christ, but that was not permitted because of her age…

[Like her brother Francisco] she deprived herself of food to give it to the poor; she did not drink water, especially in the summer heat; as a form of penance she wore a rope round her waist; she endured everything that was disagreeable in a spirit of penance and oblation…

But what cost her most was having to leave her family in order to undergo treatment in a hospital. Foreseeing that she would die… far from her dear ones at home, she said: "O my Jesus, now you can convert many sinners, because this is really a big sacrifice"…

Even in adverse and difficult circumstances, she gave witness of possessing to a high degree the theological virtues and also the virtues of prudence, justice, fortitude, temperance, humility, sincerity and modesty.'

In the Decree on Francisco, we read:

'He was sensitive to the beauty of nature… He called the sun "Our Lord's lamp" and was filled with joy at the appearance of the stars, which he named "the Angels' lamps"…

[After the apparitions of Our Lady] he had only one aspiration: to pray and suffer according to Our Lady's request. If the measure of divine benevolence towards him was extraordinary, the manner in which he wished to correspond with divine grace, in joy, fervour and constancy, was also extraordinary. He did not limit himself only to being a messenger, announcing penance and prayer, but more than that, with all his strength he conformed his life to the message which he announced, more by the goodness of works than by words…

He used to say: "How beautiful God is, how beautiful ! But he is sad because of the sins of men. I want to console him, I want to suffer for love of him"…

Every time they [the local authority] threatened him with death he replied: "If they kill us we will soon be in Heaven ! Nothing else matters!"…

He nurtured a special devotion to the Eucharist and spent much time in church, adoring the Sacrament of the Altar, which he called the "Hidden Jesus". He recited the fifteen mysteries of the Rosary daily, and many more times besides, in order to fulfil Our Lady's desire; to that he loved to add prayers and ejaculations which he had learned at the catechism classes, and which the Angel, the Most Holy Virgin and pious priests had taught him…

Docile to the precepts of the Lord and to the words of the Most Holy Virgin Mary, he progressed continually on the path of sanctity, and in a short time attained a great and solid Christian perfection.'

The miracle required for their Beatification

The miraculous cure that subsequently opened the way for their beatification, began in 1987. Emilia Santos had been paralysed for twenty-two years. She had no feeling at all from her waist downward, she suffered great pain in the upper part of her spine, she could only just move her hands and her head, and two operations and long spells in hospital had had no effect.

'During a retreat for the sick in Fatima, she began to have great devotion to the Little Shepherds, and to make continuous novenas to them. On the night of 25th March 1987, she heard a child's voice saying, "Sit up, because you can". She sat up at once without feeling any pain.' (Fr. L. Kondor, SVD, *The Seers of Fatima*).

She started to use a wheelchair, and went on with her novenas. Then, on 20th February 1989, the anniversary of Jacinta's death, she was able to stand up and walk freely and painlessly, with the help of a stick.

In 1997, the curia of Leiria conducted a diocesan investigation into the cure of Emilia Santos. It was recognised as juridically valid by the Congregation for the Causes of Saints on 21st November of the same year, and on 28th January 1999, the Medical College of the Dicastery "unanimously declared that the cure was rapid, complete, enduring and scientifically inexplicable". This was followed by a special meeting of the theologian consultors, on 7th May, and then of the ordinary session of Cardinals and Bishops, on 22nd June. At both those meetings, "doubts were settled and it was affirmed that this was a divine miracle".

Finally, on 28th June 1999, the Prefect of the Congregation for the Causes of Saints, Archbishop Saraiva Martins, presented a report of all these facts to the Holy Father, who then ordained that the decree concerning the miracle should be promulgated, and declared, in the presence of those who had been convened:

'It is evident that we have a miracle performed by God through the intercession of the Servants of God, Francisco Marto, boy, and Jacinta Marto, girl, that is, the rapid, complete and enduring cure of Maria Emilia Santos of a "paraplegia probably due to transverse myelitis of a duration of about 22 years, in the absence of psychic pathology".' (From the text of the Decree on the Miracle, translated from the Portuguese of *Voz da Fatima* of 13th July 1999, and published in *SOUL*, Nov-Dec 1999, p. 18).

Now that they are among the numbers of the Blessed, when a further miracle is confirmed to have taken place through their intercession, that is scientifically verified as inexplicable according to the laws of nature, Francisco and Jacinta will be declared Saints and worthy of public veneration throughout the universal Church.

Two months after this decree had been promulgated, the Bishop of Leiria-Fatima, Dom Serafim de Sousa Ferreira e Silva, wrote a Preface dated 21st August for the 63-page booklet, *The Spirituality of the Little Shepherds*. This work, compiled and published by Fr. Kondor in October 1999, contains two sermons which clearly illustrate the wonderful action of divine grace in the souls of Francisco and Jacinta, as well as other helpful information. In his Preface, Bishop Serafim gave the following three reasons why the Church beatifies and canonises "men and women who are brilliant examples of charity and the other evangelical virtues", taken from the Apostolic Constitution *Divinus Redemptionis Magister* of 26th January 1983:

1). *Imitation*: the Saints and Blesseds are given to us as models to imitate. Francisco and Jacinta, bearers of the message which flows from their lives, can serve as an example for the very young and for all.

2). *Veneration*: those who have been beatified can be venerated by public cult in their native country with statues on the altar and commemorative feasts. In the case of Saints the veneration extends to the universal Church.

3). *Invocation*: the Church recognises that the two children can be intercessors with God on behalf of those who invoke them.

The Bishop then went on to explain the significance of the Beatification:

'The Beatification of Francisco and Jacinta confirms or strengthens the recognition of the authenticity of the whole Fatima 'happening' from the time of the apparitions of the Angel down to the present day. And it presents the two little shepherds as the intercessors of graces and blessings for those who are still pilgrims and sinners here on earth.' (*The Spirituality of the Little Shepherds*, Preface, pp. 5, 6)

Three months later, on 11th November 1999, in an interview with *SOUL* magazine, the official organ of the American Blue Army, Bishop Serafim gave his judgment that :

'The beatification … will be a public statement from the highest authority of the Church that all the happenings of Fatima - the apparitions - are valid and authentic. There is a message, and this message corresponds to the Magisterium and to Revelation and applies to us today.' (*SOUL*, March-April 2000, p. 26)

Finally, in the course of commenting on his pilgrimage to Fatima, in his first General Audience after the Beatification on 17th May, the Holy Father stated that "with the two shepherd children of Fatima, the Church has beatified two very young people because, although they were not martyrs, they showed that they lived the Christian virtues to a heroic degree despite their young age. The heroism of children, but true heroism".

John Paul II's Homily at the Beatification Mass

In his homily at the Mass of Beatification, from which the following extracts have been taken, Pope John Paul II began by quoting the words of Jesus in the Gospel reading:

"'Father,… to you I offer praise, for what you have hidden from the learned and the clever you have revealed

to the merest children... for such was your gracious will"
(Mt 11:25, 26)...

According to the divine plan, "a woman clothed with
the sun" (Rv 12: 1) came down from heaven to this earth
to visit the privileged children of the Father. She speaks
to them with a mother's voice and heart; she asks them to
offer themselves as victims of reparation, saying that she
was ready to lead them safely to God. And behold, they
see a light shining from her maternal hands which pene-
trates them inwardly, so that they feel immersed in God
just as - they explain - a person sees himself in a mirror.

Later Francisco exclaimed:

"We were burning in that light which is God and we
were not consumed. What is God like ? It is impossible to
say. In fact we will never be able to tell people".

God: a light that burns without consuming. Moses had
the same experience when he saw God in the burning bush.

What most impressed and entirely absorbed Blessed
Francisco was God in that immense light which penetrated
the inmost depths of the three children. But God told only
Francisco "how sad" he was, as he said. One night his
father heard him sobbing, and asked him why he was cry-
ing. His son answered: "I was thinking of Jesus who is so
sad because of the sins that are committed against him".
He was motivated by one desire - so expressive of how
children think -"to console Jesus and make him happy". A
transformation takes place in his life, one we could call

radical (and) certainly uncommon for children of his age. He devotes himself to an intense spiritual life, expressed in assiduous and fervent prayer, and attains a true form of mystical union with the Lord. This spurs him to a progressive purification of the spirit through the renunciation of his own pleasures and even of innocent childhood games.

Francisco bore without complaining the great sufferings caused by the illness from which he died. It all seemed to him too little to console Jesus: he died with a smile on his lips. Little Francisco had a great desire to atone for the offences of sinners by striving to be good and by offering his sacrifices and prayers. The life of Jacinta, his younger sister by almost two years, was motivated by these same sentiments …

4. Little Jacinta felt and personally experienced Our Lady's anguish, offering herself heroically as a victim for sinners. One day, when she and Francisco had already contracted the illness that forced them to bed, the Virgin Mary came to visit them at home, as the little one recounts: "Our Lady came to see us and said that soon she would come and take Francisco to heaven. And she asked me if I still wanted to convert more sinners. I told her yes"... Jacinta had been so deeply moved by the vision of Hell during the apparition of 13 July that no mortification or penance seemed too great to save sinners. She could well exclaim with St Paul: "I rejoice in my sufferings for your sake, and in my flesh I complete what is lacking in Christ's afflictions for the sake of his body, that is, the Church' (Col 1: 24)".

Last Sunday at the Colosseum in Rome, we commemo-
rated the many witnesses to the faith in the 20th century,
recalling the tribulations they suffered through the significant testimonies they left us ... Here in Fatima, where these
times of tribulation were foretold and Our Lady asked for
prayer and penance to shorten them, I would like to thank
heaven for the powerful witness shown in all those lives ...

I also express my gratitude to Blessed Jacinta for
sacrifices and prayers offered for the Holy Father,
whom she saw suffering greatly ...

Today Jesus' praise [of the Father] takes the solemn
form of the beatification of the little shepherds Francisco
and Jacinta. With this rite, the Church wishes to put on
the candelabrum these two candles which God lit to illumine humanity in its dark and anxious hours ...

6. My last words are for the children ... Our Lady
needs you all to console Jesus, who is sad because of the
bad things done to him; he needs your prayers and your
sacrifices for sinners.

Ask your parents and teachers to enrol you in the
"school" of Our Lady, so that she can teach you to be
like the little shepherds, who tried to do whatever she
asked them. *I tell you that "one makes more progress in
a short time of submission and dependence on Mary than
during entire years of personal initiatives, relying on
oneself alone"* (author's emphasis; cited from St Louis
de Montfort, *The True Devotion to the Blessed Virgin*

Mary, n. 155). This was how the little shepherds became saints so quickly.

A woman who gave hospitality to Jacinta in Lisbon, on hearing the very beautiful and wise advice that the little girl gave, asked who taught it to her. "It was Our Lady", she replied. Devoting themselves with total generosity to the direction of such a good Teacher, Jacinta and Francisco soon reached the heights of perfection ... May the message of their lives live on for ever to light humanity's way!' (*L'Osservatore Romano,* 17th May 2000, pp. 1, 3)

On his return to Rome, in the course of reflecting on his pilgrimage to Fatima, in his General Audience of 17th May, the Holy Father stated:

'Their holiness does not depend on the apparitions but on their fidelity and commitment in responding to the extraordinary gift they received from the Lord and from Mary most holy... Because of their fidelity to God, they are a shining example to children and adults of how to comply in a simple and generous way with the transforming action of divine grace.

A message of conversion and hope has spread from Fatima throughout the world ... which, in conformity with Christian revelation ... is the true Gospel of Christ, presented anew to our generation, particularly tried by events of the past. God's appeal to us through the Blessed

Virgin still retains all its timeliness today … let us receive the light that comes from Fatima, let us be guided by Mary. May her Immaculate Heart be our refuge and the way that leads us to Christ. May the blessed shepherd children intercede for the Church.' (*L'Osservatore Romano*, 24th May 2000, p. 11)

THE MESSAGE OF FATIMA IN THE SERVICE OF EVANGELISATION IN THE THIRD MILLENNIUM

The significance of the Family in the Message of Fatima

It is providential that in the opening century of the new millennium, God has raised up the two youngest children of a family of seven, as models of holiness for children, for families, and indeed for all; and it is also a happy coincidence that we can now read a movingly intimate account of the profoundly Christian life that Sister Lucia led as a child in the home of her parents, and which she has vividly recalled in two new additions to her Memoirs, published in an English translation in 1999 by Fr. L. Kondor of the Postulation Centre, as volume II of *Fatima in Lucia's Own Words*.

These developments are providential because they have come at a time when Christianity in general is suffering a period of decline in the West, and the values of Christian family life in particular are under attack from many directions. As the Pope wrote, in his *Letter to Families* of February 1994, "the history of mankind, the history of salvation, passes by way of the family. In these pages I have tried to show how the family is placed at the centre of the great struggle between good and evil, between life and death, between love and all that is opposed to love"

(*Letter to Families*, No. 23). And in his great Encyclical on "the Value and Inviolability of Human Life" of March 1995, he taught that "the deepest roots of the struggle between the 'culture of life' and the 'culture of death' ..." lie in "the eclipse of the sense of God and of man ... at the heart of the moral conscience ... with all its various and deadly consequences for life" (*Evangelium Vitae*, No. 24).

As the influence of materialism and secularism increases, it is steadily becoming more evident that a considerable section of society today effectively treats God as if he no longer exists, to the extent that his laws and commandments are becoming progressively detached from public and private life, belief in Christ is denied, and the teaching of the Church rejected.

In the message of Fatima, Our Lady warned of these errors and the threat they pose to man's salvation, as the Holy Father stated, in the following remarks in his General Audience on returning to Rome from Fatima in May 1982:

'The threat on the part of the forces of evil comes particularly from the errors that have been spread in this very century of ours, errors based on the denial of God, and the attempt to cut off mankind completely from him, positing human life without God and even against God. In the very heart of the message that came from Fatima at the beginning of our century, we find a powerful warning about these errors. (*L'Osservatore Romano*, 24th May 1982)

Can the Mother, who with all the force of the love that she fosters in the Holy Spirit, desires everyone's salvation, keep silence on what undermines the very bases of their salvation ? No, she cannot...'

the Holy Father had exclaimed, a few days previously, in his homily at Fatima on 13th May.

In response to this threat, Our Lady came to the three youngest children of two families in Fatima, to manifest anew God's limitless love and mercy for all mankind. As we have seen above, in the Holy Father's homily at the Beatification of Francisco and Jacinta, and in the Decree on their heroic virtues, the marvellous events that then unfolded in the lives of the three shepherd children through the apparitions of the most Holy Virgin, undoubtedly constitute "a genuine help in understanding the Gospel and living it better" at this particular moment in time.

For these events are permeated with the appealing spirit of children, their spontaneous, unquestioning enthusiasm and vitality, and hence they draw us to look afresh at the fundamental truths of the Gospel and the divine mysteries of the Catholic Faith, which the little shepherds embraced so wholeheartedly. As the Holy Father said, "because of their fidelity to God, they are a shining example to children and adults of how to comply in a simple and generous way with the transforming action of divine grace" (General Audience, 24/5/00). To follow their example will be to set out on the path to holiness which is our vocation as Christians. In so doing, it will also serve as a response, both to the Holy Father's call for holiness as the primary objective of pastoral initiatives (*Novo Millennio Ineunte*, No. 30), and to the crisis of values in society today, whose root cause and animating spirit lies in the errors of the denial and rejection of God about which Our Lady warned at Fatima.

However, we must remember that the holiness they attained, was due not to their exceptional privilege in experiencing the apparitions, but to the same virtues that all are called to practice in their daily Christian life, namely, "their fidelity and commitment in responding to the extraordinary gift they received from the Lord and from Mary Most Holy" (General Audience, 24th May 2000). By Baptism, all have received the unique gift from the Lord which makes us members of his mystical body, the Church, open to receiving Jesus Himself in the Eucharist, his word in the sacred Scriptures, and the Holy Spirit in Confirmation. With the gift of the sacraments, we have the means at our disposal to respond to the Lord's call to become holy, and in the lives of Blessed Francisco and Jacinta, we have the touching example of two shepherd children to inspire us to do so.

Let us now consider how the apparitions of the Angel in 1916 initiated the children into the central theme of the message communicated by Our Lady in the following year: that God calls us to sanctify ourselves by showing our love for him, in response to his infinite love and mercy for all mankind, through the love which we show our neighbour, by offering prayers, penance, sacrifices and above all Eucharistic reparation, to obtain the conversion of sinners and the salvation of souls at risk of being lost.

The Apparitions of the Angel in 1916

In 1916, the Angel of Peace appeared three times to prepare the little shepherds for the coming of Our Lady. In his first apparition, the Angel taught them a prayer, the first part of which - "My God, I believe, I adore, I hope and I love you" - expresses the ordinary duty of all baptised Christians, to love God with all our heart and soul and mind (Mt 22: 37-39). In repeating this prayer in the second part - "I ask pardon for those who do not believe, do not adore, do not hope and do not love you" - the second commandment is likewise fulfilled, since the prayer is offered out of loving concern for those of our neighbours whose salvation is at risk, in so far as they no longer accept Christian teaching and values, and live as if there is no God.

In his second apparition, the Angel asked the children to "make of everything you can a sacrifice", to be offered to God in reparation for sin and the conversion of sinners. These words, said Sister Lucia, "were like a light which made us understand who God is, how he loves us and desires to be loved", and how sacrifices move him to grant the conversion of sinners.

In the third apparition, the Angel knelt beside the children in front of a sacred host suspended in the air, from which drops of blood fell into a chalice. In a moving prayer, the Angel offered to the Most Holy Trinity the Eucharistic presence of Jesus "in all the tabernacles of the world, in reparation for the outrages, sacrileges and indifference with which he Himself is offended". Then he gave the host to Lucia, and shared the chalice between Francisco and Jacinta, exhorting them to repair men's crimes and "console your God".

Our Lady's apparition of 13th May

The key to the unfolding of grace that subsequently ensued in the lives of the little shepherds, lies in their response to the following question that the beautiful Lady from heaven addressed to them, in her first apparition of 13th May. Note how the Holy Virgin is careful to respect the freedom of their response.

"Are you willing to offer yourselves to God and bear all the sufferings he wills to send you, as an act of reparation for the conversion of sinners ?"

"Yes, we are willing."

"Then you are going to have much to suffer, but the grace of God will be your comfort."

For the three little shepherds, this moment was the point of their conversion; and conversion, in the sense of using the freedom God has given every person to decide whether or not to accept the path that he proposes, is also the key to the significance of Our Lady's message in relation to the Church's mission of evangelisation at the present time, according to the teaching that we have been considering in this study.

As we have seen, conversion followed by repentance is the Gospel nucleus of the message. Our Lady came to call souls back to their true destiny in God. But, as the lives of Blessed Francisco and Jacinta so appealingly demonstrate, this call is addressed not only to sinners and those whose salvation is at risk. It is also a call to all Christians to convert in the sense of seeking to enter more deeply into the divine mysteries of the Faith, and to live it with greater fervour and conviction, so as to co-operate with Christ and his holy Mother in the universal work of salvation. God invites us to enter into this way, but does not impose it, because he wants us to accept it freely, out of love for him and in recognition that it will lead to our spiritual growth and sanctification.

This form of conversion can be ours too, if we follow the example of the little shepherds and respond to the grace of God's appeal through his Mother with their trusting 'yes'. In the Our Father, we profess "thy will be done". Mary herself, when greeted by the Angel at the Annunciation, responded with her *fiat*: "let it be to me according to your word" (Lk

1:38). When the holy Mother of Christ asked the little shepherds if they were willing to offer themselves to God, in effect she was repeating the invitation Jesus extended to those who would become his disciples, and which God presents to us in various ways and moments throughout our life: "If any man would come after me, let him deny himself and take up his cross daily and follow me" (Lk 9: 23).

In her memoirs, Sister Lucia then went on to record the prodigious grace that the three children experienced immediately after they had offered themselves to God. In the light which then streamed from Our Lady's hands, they saw themselves "in God Who was that light, more clearly than we see ourselves in the best of mirrors. Then, moved by an interior impulse that was also communicated to us, we fell on our knees, repeating in our hearts: O most Holy Trinity, I adore You ! My God, my God, I love you in the most Blessed Sacrament".

This sublime manifestation symbolises the grace that God desires to give us, if we offer ourselves to him through His holy Mother, the "Mother of divine grace". In his General Audience of 7th May 1997, the Holy Father commented as follows, on the words Jesus spoke from the cross to the beloved disciple, John: "Behold your mother!" (Jn 19: 26-27):

'The Church's devotion to the Virgin... is based on Christ's will... The history of Christian piety teaches that

Mary is the way which leads to Christ, and that filial devotion to her takes nothing from intimacy with Jesus. Indeed, it increases it and leads to the highest levels of perfection' (cited in *Theotokos*, A Catechesis on Mary, Mother of God, by Pope John Paul II, Pauline, 2000, p. 192).

As we have seen, Francisco and Jacinta became a living example of this teaching, as they sought to do everything that the Holy Virgin asked of them. Scenes such as the Angel's prayer of Eucharistic reparation to the Most Holy Trinity in front of the sacred host suspended in the air and dripping the Precious Blood, the vision of themselves in the light of God that streamed from Our Lady's hands, Mary's Immaculate Heart surrounded by thorns, the suffering of souls in hell, the miracle of the sun, and the last apparition in October, when the children saw the Holy Family: all these manifestations help to move our hearts and convince our minds more deeply of the divine realities of the Faith.

Pilgrims to Fatima constantly bear witness, how their faith is stirred in the love of God and of his Holy Mother for us sinners, when they see the Cova da Iria, now so totally transformed, and pray in the Capelinha in front of the venerated statue of the Holy Virgin, which has been placed at the precise spot where she came to speak with the three little shepherds, and where Pope John Paul II has knelt long in silent prayer, on three separate occasions. Likewise the hill above the village of Aljustrel where the children lived, and where pilgrims throng to make the outdoor Stations of the Cross, is another area where one receives a strong sense of the supernatural, in the midst of the beauty of nature that so attracted Francisco. For here, in complete contrast to the Sanctuary, the landscape has remained almost unchanged since the time of the apparitions; and after making the Stations, one can pray in the Loca da Cabeço, at the spot where a marble monument commemorates the Angel and the children offering the moving prayer of Eucharistic reparation to the Most Holy Trinity.

Even if we cannot go on pilgrimage to Fatima, these and some of the other scenes that are encountered there leave vivid impressions in our imagination, which can assist our life of prayer, our desire to receive the sacraments, our devotion in receiving Jesus in the Eucharist, our love for his most holy Mother, and our willingness to bear our cross with fortitude.

After their first encounter with "the Lady of the message", as we have seen in the moving testimonies of their lives that have been previously cited, Blessed Francisco and Jacinta abandoned their childhood amusements, and devoting themselves "with total generosity to the direction of such a good Teacher", embraced the way of the Cross that Our Lady held out to them. As Bishop Serafim of Leiria-Fatima stated, "with great love … they lived courageously the martyrdom of misunderstanding, illness and death" (*The Spirituality of the Little Shepherds*, Preface, p. 8).

Having offered themselves willingly to God, thence-
forth Francisco and Jacinta began to change their lives as
they strove to do whatever the Holy Virgin asked of
them. The story of how Our Lady's apparitions subsequently unfolded can be read in Leo Madigan's excellent
account, *What Happened at Fatima* (CTS, 2000).
Meanwhile, in the space that remains, we will summarise
briefly three different ways in which the message of
Fatima can serve the Church's mission of evangelisation.

The sacrifice of our daily duty

Perhaps the most important point to emphasise is that Our
Lady's message helps people to strengthen their faith and
preserve it from influences which seek to undermine it,
and this can be particularly valuable for lay people, who
are called to live in the midst of an increasingly self-cen-
tred, materialistic society, that is dominated by a spirit of
godless secularism.

The basic elements of the message of Fatima - prayer,
penance, reparation, daily recitation of the Rosary, sacrifices - coincide readily with the ordinary pattern of every-
day life, and thus offer a means of serving God that is
simple to adopt and open to people in all walks of life.

The Angel urged the shepherd children to "make of
everything you can a sacrifice", in reparation for the sins
which offend God, and for the conversion of sinners.
"You will thus draw down peace upon your country". In

other words, what can be offered up to God, without any need to look for special penances, are matters arising from the ordinary circumstances and daily duties of our life, the irksome tasks that have to be done anyway, the affairs that go wrong, the unexpected suffering, the little unseen acts of self-denial from time to time. The sufferings that would be considered as losses and setbacks in human terms, can be turned into gains for souls, if we offer them up in reparation for sin, and if when we do so we say, as Our Lady asked that we should do many times, especially when we make some sacrifice: "O Jesus, it is for love of you, for the conversion of sinners, and in reparation for the sins committed against the Immaculate Heart of Mary".

Daily recitation of the Rosary

Next, while we may only be able to get to Mass on Sundays, we can recall and meditate on the divine mysteries of Christ's life through praying the Rosary, at almost any place and time. Knowing the difficult times that would come for the Faith through which we are now living, perhaps this is one reason why at Fatima the Holy Virgin laid particular emphasis on the Rosary, requesting six times in succession that it should be prayed every day. "I am the Lady of the Rosary", she revealed in her final apparition on 13th October.

More than fifty Popes have urged the faithful to pray the Rosary because through praying and meditating the mysteries of Jesus' birth, death and resurrection, the Rosary has power to overcome sin and evil, to drive away the devil, and to bring about peace and conversion of heart.

Pope St. Pius X said that "the Rosary is the most beautiful and rich in graces of all prayers… that touches most the Heart of the Mother of God… If you wish peace to reign in your homes, recite the family Rosary". Pope Paul VI stated that "as a Gospel prayer, centred on the mystery of the Redemptive Incarnation… the litany-like succession of Hail Mary's becomes in itself an unceasing praise of Christ" (*Marialis Cultus*, No. 46).

On his pilgrimage to Fatima in May 1982, Pope John Paul II said: "Take care of your inheritance of faith… Do you want me to teach you the secret of keeping it ? It is simple… Pray, pray very much, pray, recite the Rosary every day" (12th May). And in his homily at Mass on 13th, the Pope said that the Rosary "can rightly be defined as 'Mary's prayer' in which… she herself prays with us".

Finally, in his message to the Bishop of Leiria-Fatima dated 1st October 1997, the Holy Father urged the faithful to "recite the Rosary every day… for the faithful and courageous fulfilment of the human and Christian duties proper to each one's state", and later that month he quoted with approval Pius XII's description of the Rosary as "a compendium of the Gospel" (Angelus, 26th October 1997).

Here I would like to add a brief personal testimony in gratitude to Almighty God and in honour of Our Lady, in

the hope that others may be encouraged to have recourse
to God through the prayer of the Rosary. Some years after
I had been received into the Church, I began to learn of
Mary and the power before God of her Rosary. So our
family began to pray the mysteries, especially for my
father. I was concerned for his salvation since he was a
Freemason and shortly before his death had told me that
he did not accept that Christ is God. When in due course
he died, he passed away in great peace on the feast of the
Annunciation, in such marvellous circumstances that I
have always believed Our Lady intervened to save his
soul. Ten years later, my mother, who likewise had
almost no apparent belief in God, died on the vigil of the
feast of the Maternity of Mary, in similarly consoling circumstances that could only have been the fruit of prayer,
and especially, in my belief, the Rosary.

It is experiences such as these which can transcribe the
sublime truths of our holy religion more deeply into our
souls, and which the Church holds out to all who will use
the means of grace that she places at our disposal.

The Five First Saturdays devotion

Finally, in the Five First Saturdays devotion Our Lady
revealed the Eucharistic reparation that was prefigured in
the third apparition of the Angel. The devotion was first
revealed by Our Lady on 13th July 1917, in the following
words in the second part of the secret:

'...this is the great sign given you by God that he is about to punish the world for its crimes, by means of war, famine, and persecutions of the Church and of the Holy Father. To prevent this, I shall come to ask for the consecration of Russia to my Immaculate Heart, and the Communion of Reparation on the First Saturdays.'

The importance of the devotion is such that it is linked with the act of consecration by the Holy Father (the act which Pope John Paul II carried out at Rome on 25th March 1984), as the means to prevent God punishing the world for its crimes.

The precise nature of the devotion was subsequently revealed on 10th December 1925, when the Holy Virgin appeared to Lucia, with the Holy Child at her side and showing her Heart encircled by thorns. The Holy Child said:

'Have compassion on the Heart of your most holy Mother, covered with thorns, with which ungrateful men pierce it at every moment, and there is no one to make an act of reparation to remove them.'

The Holy Virgin then said:

'Look, my daughter, at my Heart surrounded with thorns with which ungrateful men pierce me at every moment by their blasphemies and ingratitude. You at least try to console me and say that I promise to assist at the hour of death, with the graces necessary for salvation, all those who, on the first Saturday of five consecutive months, shall confess, receive Holy Communion, recite five decades of the Rosary, and keep me company for fifteen minutes while meditating on the fifteen mysteries of the Rosary, with the intention of making reparation to me.'

In a letter dated 12th June 1930, Sister Lucia revealed that Jesus had told her that confession within eight days of the First Saturday would suffice, provided that the Communion is made in a state of grace and with the intention of making reparation to the Immaculate Heart of Mary. The devotion was to be practised on the first Saturdays of five consecutive months, in reparation for the five kinds of offences and blasphemies uttered against Our Lady which required reparation. These were: blasphemies against the Immaculate Conception, against Our Lady's virginity, against her divine maternity and the refusal to recognise her as mother of men, blasphemies by those seeking to alienate children from her, and in reparation for those who outrage Our Lady in her sacred images.

Conclusion

As we have seen, the message of Fatima is an appeal from the Heart of the Mother, in her deep concern for the salvation of all the human family, for "today as never before in the past, humanity stands at a crossroads".

Today indeed as never before, Christ and the Gospel are being challenged even in the most intimate sanctuary of the very human life itself that God has created in his own image and likeness, in an unprecedented spirit of violation and denial of his laws, and rejection of his presence. In opposition to the "civilisation of love" that Christ wills to establish on earth, there has arisen a "culture of death". At Fatima, Mary Most Holy came to reaffirm the presence of God, and to warn us of these errors, whose true nature and the grave consequences they entail for society have been clearly set out in the teaching of Pope John Paul II, most notably in his Encyclical, *Evangelium Vitae*.

Today as never before, no practising Christian can afford to be indifferent to the threat posed by these counter-Gospel values. By his rebellion against God, through the increasingly grave deviations from the divine and natural law that we see all around us, man continues to raise against himself the flaming sword of judgment held over the world by the Angel, in the third part of the secret of Fatima.

In response to this threat, in her serene spirit of total self-offering to and ardent love of God, the most Holy Virgin comes to present us with an invitation, which offers us the sacramental and spiritual means, if we choose to respond to her requests, to fulfil our calling as Christians to be sanctified, and in doing so, to work for the salvation of those in society who "do not believe, do not adore, do not hope and do not love you".

With this intention, in the message of Fatima the Mother continues to repeat to all who come to hear it, the question she first put to Francisco and Jacinta:

"Are you willing to offer yourselves to God… ?"

God is waiting for us to respond to the marvellous outpouring of love and mercy he has shown for mankind through his holy Mother at Fatima, by freely showing our love for him in return. In making our response to her invitation, may the Immaculate Heart of Mary enlighten us, and be the way that leads us to Christ.